Anime coloring book for kids

age 4 - 8

age 8 - 12

Author: Charlie S. McTony

Thank you.

We hope you enjoyed our book.

As a small family company, your feedback is very important to us.

Please let us know how you like our book at:

adrian.stoica@deannaosc.com